CLEVELAND
BROWNS

by Marty Gitlin

Published by ABDO Publishing Company, 8000 West 78th Street, Edina, Minnesota 55439. Copyright © 2011 by Abdo Consulting Group, Inc. International copyrights reserved in all countries. No part of this book may be reproduced in any form without written permission from the publisher. SportsZone™ is a trademark and logo of ABDO Publishing Company.

Printed in the United States of America,
North Mankato, Minnesota
062010
092010

Editor: Matt Tustison
Copy Editor: Nicholas Cafarelli
Interior Design and Production: Kazuko Collins
Cover Design: Kazuko Collins

Photo Credits: Paul Abell/AP Images, cover; NFL Photos/AP Images, title page, 7, 29, 30, 44; AP Images, 4, 9, 10, 13, 15, 18, 20, 23, 25, 42 (top), 42 (bottom), 43 (top); Harold P. Matosian/AP Images, 17, 42 (middle); Mark Duncan/AP Images, 26, 33, 41, 43 (middle); Ted Mathias/AP Images, 34; Tony Dejak/AP Images, 37, 38, 43 (bottom); Paul M. Walsh/AP Images, 47

Library of Congress Cataloging-in-Publication Data
Gitlin, Marty.
  Cleveland Browns / Marty Gitlin.
     p. cm. — (Inside the NFL)
  Includes index.
  ISBN 978-1-61714-008-2
  1. Cleveland Browns (Football team : 1946-1995)—Juvenile literature. 2. Cleveland Browns (Football team : 1999-)—History—Juvenile literature. I. Title.
  GV956.C6G58 2011
  796.332'640977132—dc22
                                    2010014043

TABLE OF CONTENTS

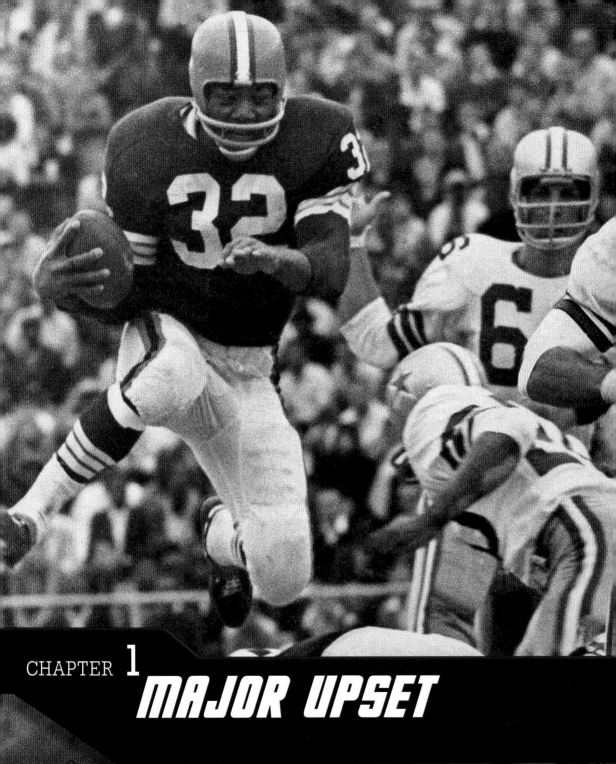

CHAPTER 1

MAJOR UPSET

Nobody believed that the Cleveland Browns would defeat the mighty Baltimore Colts in the 1964 National Football League (NFL) Championship Game. That is, nobody but the Cleveland Browns.

The Colts were downright scary. They boasted a 12–2 record and had won 12 of their previous 13 games.

Baltimore's offense was led by Johnny Unitas, the finest quarterback in the NFL. The team's defense had given up seven points or fewer in five separate games.

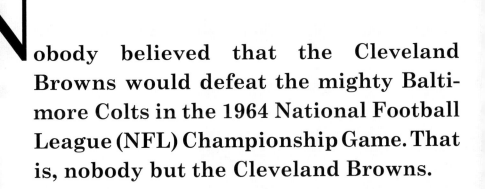

WHOOPS!

Sports Illustrated certainly goofed as the 1964 NFL title game approached. Its editors were so certain of the outcome that they placed photos of Baltimore coach Don Shula and quarterback Johnny Unitas on the cover before the game was even played! When the Browns upset the Colts, the magazine's editors had to scramble to fix their mistake. They redid the cover with a picture of Cleveland quarterback Frank Ryan.

THE BROWNS AND JIM BROWN, SHOWN IN A 1964 REGULAR-SEASON CONTEST, WERE READY TO LEAP INTO ACTION AGAINST THE COLTS IN THAT YEAR'S NFL TITLE GAME.

GREATEST PLAYER EVER?

The debate has raged for decades: Who is the best player in NFL history? A small number of stars are generally mentioned. And Pro Football Hall of Fame running back Jim Brown is almost always in the mix.

Drafted by the Browns out of Syracuse University in 1957, Brown dominated the NFL from the start. He led the league in rushing yards as a rookie and in eight of the nine seasons he played.

Brown ran for an NFL-record 1,863 yards in 1963, a mark that stood for a decade. His single-season average of 6.4 yards per attempt that year remained the best in league history through 2009.

Some of Brown's other records have since been broken. It has been speculated that Brown would still hold many of them had he not retired at age 29 to pursue an acting career.

The Browns, on the other hand? They had played well in the regular season. But they were far from dominant. They had lost three games and tied another. Their defense was average at best. It is no wonder that they were given little chance to beat the Colts.

The showdown was two days after Christmas. A bitterly cold wind whipped around Cleveland Municipal Stadium. Both offenses struggled early. In fact, the score at halftime was still 0–0. The Browns were encouraged.

After all, their defense had shut out Unitas and the powerful Colts for one half. If they could get their own passing attack and sensational running back Jim Brown jump-started, they could win the championship.

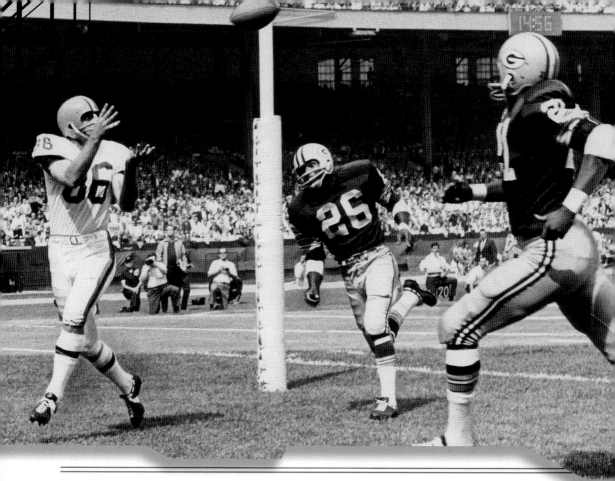

CLEVELAND WIDE RECEIVER GARY COLLINS, SHOWN IN THE 1966 SEASON, WAS A KEY PLAYER IN THE 1964 NFL CHAMPIONSHIP GAME.

That is exactly what happened. The combination of quarterback Frank Ryan and wide receiver Gary Collins got rolling. The two hooked up on touchdown strikes of 18 and 42 yards to give the Browns a 17–0 lead in the third quarter.

STEPPING UP

Browns wide receiver Gary Collins had one of his worst seasons in 1964. He caught just 35 passes all year. But in the title game, Collins excelled. His success seemed to boost his confidence, and Collins blossomed. He compiled nearly 1,000 receiving yards and earned Pro Bowl team spots in 1965 and 1966. He averaged 10 touchdowns per season from 1963 to 1967.

The Browns had the momentum, and they ran away with it. A 51-yard Ryan-to-Collins scoring pass made it 27–0. Meanwhile, Brown was running wild. What had been a mediocre defense all season limited Unitas to 95 passing yards and even intercepted two of his throws.

"We had a collective attitude that nobody was going to beat us," offensive guard Jim Houston said. "That is a remarkable feeling."

> **"We had a collective attitude that nobody was going to beat us. That is a remarkable feeling."**
> —Browns offensive guard Jim Houston, on the team's 27–0 win over the Colts in the 1964 NFL title game

And when the final tick went off the clock in the Browns' 27–0 victory, many in the crowd of almost 80,000 rushed onto the field and tore down the goalposts.

They had no way of knowing that more than 40 years later, Cleveland fans would still be waiting to celebrate another title.

BROWNS QUARTERBACK FRANK RYAN GIVES A SALUTE AFTER CLEVELAND'S 27–0 WIN OVER BALTIMORE IN THE 1964 NFL CHAMPIONSHIP GAME.

CHAPTER 2

FAST START

The Browns' upset win over the Colts in the 1964 NFL Championship Game excited fans in Cleveland. But they were used to celebrating titles. The Browns were founded as a member of the All-America Football Conference (AAFC). The league existed for four seasons, from 1946 through 1949. The Browns won the title each year. Their record was 52–4–3 during that time.

It is well known that the 1972 Miami Dolphins were the only team to have ever completed an NFL championship season undefeated. The Dolphins went 14–0 in the regular season. Then they won three playoff games, including Super Bowl VII, to finish 17–0.

But few are aware that the Browns accomplished that same feat in the AAFC in 1948. They won all 14 regular-season games and capped off their incredible run by clobbering the Buffalo Bills 49–7 in the title clash.

WITH QUARTERBACK OTTO GRAHAM AND COACH PAUL BROWN LEADING THE WAY, THE BROWNS MADE A VERY SUCCESSFUL TRANSITION FROM THE AAFC TO THE NFL.

However, when the AAFC folded and the Browns were accepted into the NFL, the skeptics had a field day. They claimed that the team from Cleveland would be destroyed by the established clubs from a superior league. The Browns got an early test playing the defending champion Philadelphia Eagles in the first game of the 1950 season.

NFL fans buzzed with anticipation. They could not wait to hear about how the upstart Browns were drubbed by the powerful Eagles. While the Browns were dominating the AAFC, George Preston Marshall, owner of the NFL's Washington Redskins, was asked what he thought about the AAFC. "The worst team in our league could beat the best team in theirs," he said.

Browns coach Paul Brown never joined the war of words. He bided his time. And on September 16, 1950, his team had a chance to silence the critics.

The Browns did not just win. They thrashed the stunned Eagles 35–10. Hall of Fame

BROWN'S BROWNS

The history of the Cleveland Browns begins with Paul Brown. He ran the organization and named it after himself. Brown styled the team's uniforms and affixed no logo to the orange helmets. The Browns remain the only team in the NFL with a plain helmet. He pioneered the use of playbooks. This resulted in more complex offenses and defenses. It also made it harder for other teams to prepare for games against the Browns. He began the practice of studying footage of opponents to construct a better game plan for his team. He also started the signing of full-time assistant coaches and African-American players. Owner Art Modell created plenty of protest when he fired Brown as coach after the 1962 season. Brown entered the Pro Football Hall of Fame in 1967. In 1968, he returned to the sideline as owner, general manager, and coach of the expansion Cincinnati Bengals.

MAC SPEEDIE CARRIES THE BALL DURING CLEVELAND'S STUNNING 35–10
WIN OVER PHILADELPHIA ON SEPTEMBER 16, 1950.

quarterback Otto Graham threw for 346 yards and three touchdowns—one each to receivers Dub Jones, Dante Lavelli, and Mac Speedie.

Brown did not reply to those who claimed his team played inferior football. Instead, he placed newspaper clippings filled with their quotes on the team's bulletin board. Those clippings inspired his team to prove the critics wrong.

"For four years, Coach Brown never said a word; he just kept putting that stuff on the bulletin board," Graham said. "We were so fired up; we would have played [the Eagles] anywhere, anytime, for a keg of beer or a chocolate milkshake. It didn't matter."

"THE TOE"

Some Browns fans remember Lou "The Toe" Groza only as a chubby place-kicker. True, he booted many important field goals near the end of his career. But Groza, who wore his familiar number 76 uniform for most of his career, was among the finest offensive linemen in the game from 1948 to 1959. He even earned the NFL Player of the Year award in 1954. Through 2009, he still held the NFL record with five seasons leading the league in field goals. When he left the sport in 1968, he had scored 1,608 points—more than any player in NFL history. It is no wonder that the address of the Browns' headquarters is 76 Lou Groza Boulevard.

The Browns steamrolled through the NFL just as they did the AAFC. Their opponents no longer took Graham's bunch lightly.

Lou Groza was the hero in the 1950 title game. He kicked a field goal with 28 seconds left to clinch a 30–28 win over the Los Angeles Rams. The Browns then embarked on a period of dominance never before seen in the NFL. They reached the championship game in six consecutive seasons and won three crowns.

Perhaps the most satisfying victory came in 1954. The Browns had lost in the 1952 and 1953 NFL finals to the Detroit Lions. But they achieved revenge in the 1954 title game. In fact, the outcome was all but decided when they sprinted to a 35–10

CLEVELAND'S STAR RUNNING BACK MARION MOTLEY WAS ONE OF THE FIRST AFRICAN-AMERICAN PLAYERS IN PROFESSIONAL FOOTBALL.

BRILLIANT BACKS

The Browns were long known for their superb running backs. The first was a 232-pound bruiser named Marion Motley. Motley was among the top four rushers in the AAFC during all four years of its existence, and he led the league in 1948. By the time the Browns were absorbed into the NFL, he was 30 years old and had two failing knees. But he just picked up where he left off, winning that league's rushing title in 1950.

In the early 1960s, though, tragedy hit the Browns at the running back spot. In 1961, they obtained a superb running back named Ernie Davis. He had been drafted that year by the Washington Redskins, who traded him to Cleveland. Davis had followed in Jim Brown's footsteps at the University of Syracuse and seemed to be on the verge of greatness. But he never played in the NFL. He contracted leukemia and died in the summer of 1962.

halftime lead. The Browns cruised to a 56–10 thumping of the Lions. Graham led the way, passing for three touchdowns and running for three more.

The biggest heroes, however, performed for Cleveland's defense. They set an NFL Championship Game record by intercepting six passes against Detroit Hall of Fame quarterback Bobby Layne. The Browns added three fumble recoveries.

"I saw it, but still hardly can believe it," Lions coach Buddy Parker exclaimed after the game. "It has me dazed."

Graham went out with a bang the next year. He retired after leading the Browns to yet another title. This one was clinched with a 38–14 victory over the Rams in the NFL Championship Game.

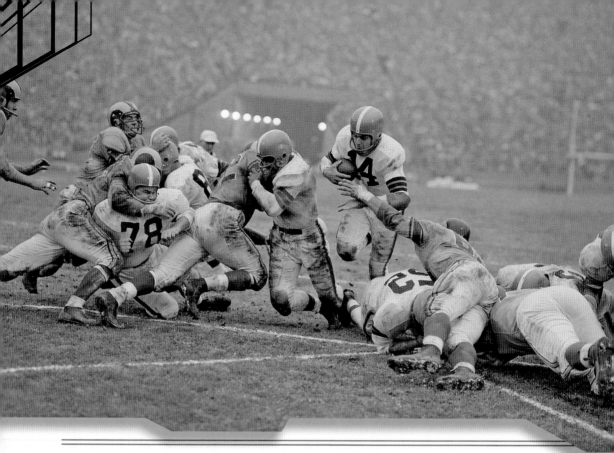

OTTO GRAHAM SCORES IN THE FINAL CONTEST OF HIS CAREER—THE BROWNS' 38–14 WIN OVER THE RAMS IN THE 1955 NFL TITLE GAME.

Despite Graham's departure, the Browns continued to win. They played for the title in 1957 and won it in 1964. They eventually declined. But not before they flirted with Super Bowl berths twice in the late 1960s.

BETWEEN GRAHAM AND BROWN

Hall of Fame quarterback Otto Graham retired after the 1955 season. Hall of Fame running back Jim Brown joined the team in 1957. Where did that leave the Browns in 1956? That was their only losing season between 1946 and 1973. They finished 5–7 that year. They returned to the NFL title game when Brown was a rookie and did not suffer through another losing year until 1974.

CHAPTER 3
END OF GREATNESS

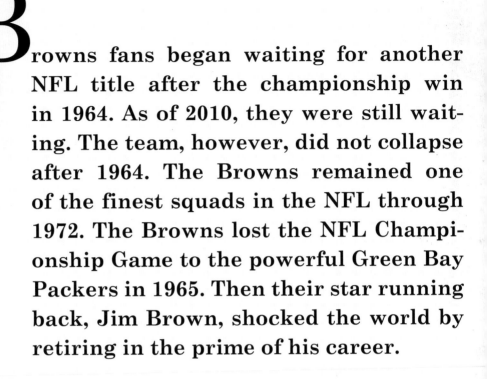

Browns fans began waiting for another NFL title after the championship win in 1964. As of 2010, they were still waiting. The team, however, did not collapse after 1964. The Browns remained one of the finest squads in the NFL through 1972. The Browns lost the NFL Championship Game to the powerful Green Bay Packers in 1965. Then their star running back, Jim Brown, shocked the world by retiring in the prime of his career.

The Browns then unveiled their third Hall of Fame running back in a row. Leroy Kelly picked up where Brown left off.

Kelly helped Cleveland make its way into the playoffs five times in a six-year span ending in 1972. He led the team to upset victories over the Dallas Cowboys in the first rounds of the 1968 and 1969 playoffs.

CLEVELAND RUNNING BACK JIM BROWN LOOKS ON DURING A GAME IN 1965. BROWN, STILL IN HIS PRIME, RETIRED AFTER THE SEASON.

VIKINGS DEFENDERS TOPPLE THE BROWNS' LEROY KELLY IN THE NFL CHAMPIONSHIP GAME ON JANUARY 4, 1969. CLEVELAND LOST 27–7.

THE OLD SWITCHEROO

The 1970 merger of the American Football League (AFL) and National Football League (NFL) affected the Browns greatly. The new arrangement divided the NFL into the American Football Conference (AFC) and National Football Conference (NFC). But three of the NFL teams had to agree to join the AFC to give each conference an even number of teams. Browns owner Art Modell asked for his team to be one of them. The Browns have played in the AFC ever since.

The Browns were on the verge of qualifying for the Super Bowl. The game was created in 1967 and pitted the NFL champion against the winner of the upstart American Football League. But the Browns lost NFL title games against the Baltimore Colts in 1968 and the Minnesota Vikings in 1969 by a combined score of 61–7.

Owner Art Modell decided to make a bold move—but it resulted in disaster. After the 1969 season, he traded Hall of Fame wide receiver Paul Warfield for the rights to draft quarterback Mike Phipps. Phipps failed miserably. So did the Browns.

Phipps seemed promising at first. He led the team into the playoffs and a near upset of unbeaten Miami in 1972. But two years later, the Browns suffered through the second losing season in their history.

Cleveland then lost its first nine games in 1975. The Browns recovered during the rest of the decade to play decent football. However, it was not until a handsome, curly-haired quarterback arrived that the Browns gave their fans hope.

LIGHTS, CAMERA, ACTION!

The Browns kicked off *Monday Night Football* at Municipal Stadium on September 21, 1970, with a 31–21 win over the New York Jets.

The first-ever Monday night game featured two major highlights. One was a 94-yard kickoff return for a Cleveland touchdown to open the second half by newly acquired Homer Jones. The other was the performance of Browns quarterback Bill Nelsen, who outplayed legendary counterpart Joe Namath.

"I remember we stayed in the same hotel as the Jets that day," Nelsen recalled. "We're going out the door and Namath's being swamped by all the fans for autographs, and I just walked through and nobody noticed me. . . . My mother ended up writing a letter to [*Monday Night Football* announcer] Howard Cosell, saying, 'Do you know who won the game? All you talked about was Namath.'"

That quarterback was Brian Sipe. In 1980, Sipe led the Browns on perhaps their most magical run. He guided the team to a series of heart-stopping comeback victories.

The thrilling games the young Browns played every Sunday earned them the nickname "The Kardiac Kids." And the fans could hardly contain their joy when their team earned a playoff spot.

THE "WIZARD OF OZ"

The Browns hit the jackpot in the 1978 college draft. Not only did they select talented linebacker Clay Matthews, but they also picked a wide receiver out of the University of Alabama named Ozzie Newsome. Then they converted him to tight end. That turned out to be a good call. Newsome developed into one of the premier pass-catchers in the history of the NFL. He set what was then a league record for a tight end with 662 receptions and landed in the Pro Football Hall of Fame.

The windchill factor was minus 36 on January 4, 1981. Nearly 80,000 fans bundled up to watch their beloved Browns play the Oakland Raiders in the frigid cold.

The Browns trailed 14–12 with just a few minutes remaining. But Sipe and running back Mike Pruitt led a charge downfield. They reached Oakland's 13-yard line.

Browns coach Sam Rutigliano had to make a decision. Should he send out kicker Don Cockroft to attempt to win the game with a field goal? It would be only 30 yards. But the wind was howling, the snow was falling, and Cockroft had been struggling.

Rutigliano was a gambler. He decided that he would try for

QUARTERBACK BRIAN SIPE LED THE BROWNS TO SEVERAL COMEBACK WINS IN 1980, EARNING THEM THE NICKNAME "THE KARDIAC KIDS."

a touchdown. He called for a play known as "Red Right 88"—words that still sting Browns fans everywhere. Sipe fired a pass into the end zone to sure-handed tight end Ozzie Newsome. But it was intercepted by the Raiders' Mike Davis. The game was lost. You could hear a pin drop at Municipal Stadium.

"We've lived and died with the pass all year long," Newsome said in the gloomy Browns locker room. "This time we died."

> ## "We've lived and died with the pass all year long. This time we died."
> —Browns tight end Ozzie Newsome, on the team's 14–12 playoff loss to the Raiders in January 1981

The Browns died for a while. They did not recover until another quarterback hero arrived in 1985. And this one came right from their own backyard.

ARE THEY RELATED?

Greg Pruitt and Mike Pruitt are not related. But one followed the other as a highly successful running back for the Browns. Greg was small but strong and quick. He rushed for more than 1,000 yards in 1975, 1976, and 1977. By that time, Mike was ready to take over. Mike Pruitt emerged with 1,294 yards and nine touchdowns in 1979 and eclipsed the 1,000-yard mark in three of the next four seasons too.

OAKLAND'S MIKE DAVIS INTERCEPTS A PASS INTENDED FOR CLEVELAND'S OZZIE NEWSOME ON THE "RED RIGHT 88" PLAY ON JANUARY 4, 1981.

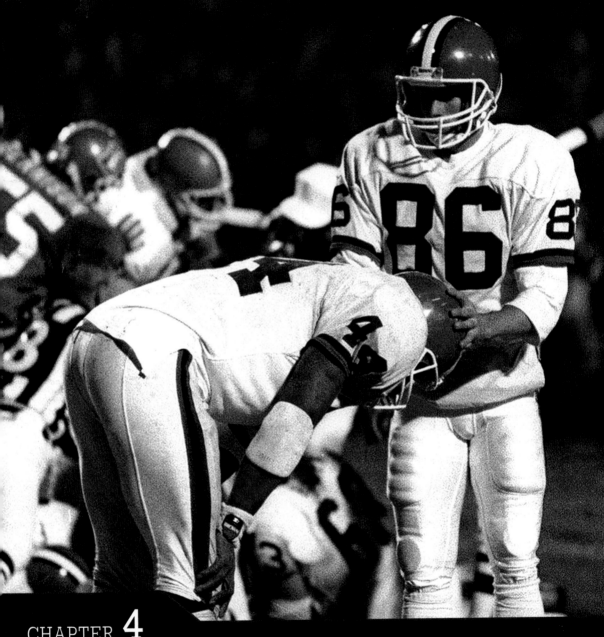

CHAPTER 4

SO CLOSE, YET SO FAR

Bernie Kosar looked funny tossing a football. He threw it almost sidearm. He was slow and awkward. Yet he found success because of his intelligence and accuracy.

When Kosar was growing up in nearby Youngstown, Ohio, he was a big Browns fan. After a stellar career at the University of Miami in Florida, he was taken by his hometown team in the 1985 supplemental draft.

That selection launched a period of excellence for the Browns. They qualified for the playoffs in each of the next five years.

ELITE COMPANY

Through 2009, an NFL team featured two 1,000-yard rushers in the same season only six times. Miami's Larry Csonka and Mercury Morris achieved that distinction in 1972, and Pittsburgh's Franco Harris and Rocky Bleier did the same four years later. The Browns' Earnest Byner and Kevin Mack accomplished that feat in 1985. Mack rushed for 1,104 yards and Byner added 1,002 that season. It was 21 years until it was done again, by Atlanta's Michael Vick and Warrick Dunn.

THE BROWNS' BRIAN BRENNAN, *RIGHT*, COMFORTS EARNEST BYNER AFTER HE FUMBLED LATE IN THE AFC CHAMPIONSHIP GAME ON JANUARY 17, 1988.

"THE DAWGS"

In the summer of 1985, Browns cornerback Hanford Dixon coined a nickname for the team's defense that is still used today.

"We didn't have a great defensive line, and I was just thinking of a way to get those guys going," he explained. "I started barking at them. The fans . . . were so close to the [practice] fields, they'd hear me and [fellow cornerback Frank Minnifield] barking, and they'd bark back." Dixon decided to call the defense "The Dawgs." He even placed a banner in the bleachers at Municipal Stadium that proclaimed it "The Dawg Pound."

Dixon and Minnifield made the new nickname popular by barking during radio and television interviews. They also backed up their bravado on the field. During the second half of the 1980s, no cornerback combination in the NFL proved more effective in covering receivers.

The Browns had developed a fine team. Kosar had plenty of weapons on which to rely, including running backs Earnest Byner and Kevin Mack and tight end Ozzie Newsome. The defense featured a strong secondary led by cornerbacks Hanford Dixon and Frank Minnifield. Clay Matthews was among the top linebackers in the sport.

The Browns reached the AFC title game after the 1986, 1987, and 1989 seasons. But they lost all three to the Denver Broncos. The most frustrating defeat was the first one. Playing in front of their passionate fans, the Browns forged ahead 20–13 on a touchdown pass from Kosar to

A FAN CHEERS IN "THE DAWG POUND" SECTION AT CLEVELAND'S MUNICIPAL STADIUM DURING A PLAYOFF GAME AFTER THE 1987 SEASON.

Brian Brennan with less than six minutes remaining.

Those remaining minutes were all that stood between the Browns and their first Super Bowl berth. But Denver quarterback John Elway engineered a 98-yard touchdown drive that tied the score, and the Browns lost 23–20 in overtime.

"The whole game, we were talking on defense of going to the Super Bowl," Browns linebacker Eddie Johnson said afterward in a glum locker room. "There's no way I will be able to sleep tonight."

The Browns lost another heartbreaker in the AFC title game a year later, this time in Denver. They were on their way to a game-tying touchdown when Byner fumbled on the Broncos' 3-yard line to seal Denver's victory.

THRILLER!

Perhaps the most exciting game in Browns history occurred in the first round of the playoffs against the New York Jets on January 3, 1987. The Jets led 20–10 with just four minutes remaining. The Browns appeared doomed. But they scored a touchdown with less than two minutes left and made a field goal with just seconds remaining to tie the score and send the game into overtime. Place-kicker Mark Moseley, who missed an easy 23-yard field-goal attempt in the first overtime period, then won it with a 27-yarder in the second overtime for a 23–20 victory.

"The whole game, we were talking on defense of going to the Super Bowl. There's no way I will be able to sleep tonight."
—Browns linebacker Eddie Johnson, on Cleveland's 23–20 overtime loss to Denver in the AFC title game in January 1987

CLEVELAND QUARTERBACK BERNIE KOSAR THREW THE BALL IN AN UNUSUAL WAY, BUT HE WAS VERY SUCCESSFUL.

Though the Browns reached the doorstep of a Super Bowl again in 1989, they have never truly recovered.

When the Browns released Kosar in 1993, the fans were outraged—despite the fact that the team was in the midst of its fourth consecutive losing season. He subsequently signed with Dallas. Kosar was replaced at quarterback by Vinny Testaverde, who helped the Browns reach the playoffs in 1994.

By that time, however, owner Art Modell was showing signs of discontent. He was angry that the city of Cleveland had agreed to build a new baseball stadium for the Indians and a basketball arena for the Cavaliers.

Modell waited in vain for a new football stadium for his Browns. But few could have predicted what he did in 1995.

DRAFT-DAY DISASTER

In the spring of 1987, the Browns traded premier linebacker Chip Banks for the rights to draft Duke University standout Mike Junkin, who was to be his replacement at that position. It was arguably the worst draft-day move in team history. Coach Marty Schottenheimer was glowing in his remarks about Junkin, calling him "a mad dog in a meat market." Junkin performed so poorly that he was out of the NFL by 1989.

THE BROWNS' CHRIS ROCKINS (37) AND RAY ELLIS TACKLE THE BRONCOS' GERALD WILLHITE IN THE AFC TITLE GAME IN JANUARY 1987.

CHAPTER 5

MISERY, THEN MORE MISERY

It was November 6, 1995. Browns fans awoke that morning to see owner Art Modell on television. They feared the worst, and they were right. He was moving the franchise to Baltimore. Modell had been upset that a new stadium had not been built for his team to replace Municipal Stadium, which was old and creaky. He at least wanted millions of dollars spent to repair the old stadium.

When Modell's complaints went unheeded, he negotiated a deal with Baltimore to bring the Browns there. And on that fall morning, he made it official, criticizing Cleveland leaders in the process.

TITLE IN BALTIMORE

When the Browns moved to Baltimore after the 1995 season, they became known as the Baltimore Ravens. The Ravens inherited the Browns' players but were considered a new team. Led by linebacker Ray Lewis, drafted in 1996, Baltimore improved quickly. The improvement was so swift that the 2000 Ravens reached the Super Bowl and won it, 34–7 over the New York Giants.

BROWNS OWNER ART MODELL ACKNOWLEDGES A CROWD IN BALTIMORE ON NOVEMBER 6, 1995. MODELL ANNOUNCED THAT HIS TEAM WAS MOVING TO THAT CITY FROM CLEVELAND.

JOSH CRIBBS

Who has been the best Browns player since the team came back to Cleveland in 1999? The likely choice might not be a starter on offense or defense. It might be Josh Cribbs, who just might be the best kick returner in the history of the NFL.

Cribbs played quarterback at Kent State University in Ohio and was not even drafted. The Browns signed him as a free agent in 2005.

The speedy and elusive Cribbs returned three kickoffs for touchdowns in 2009. That gave him eight in his career, which set an all-time NFL record. And he achieved it in just five seasons. Through 2009, Cribbs had returned at least one kickoff for a touchdown in each season that he had been in the league.

Cribbs earned a spot on the All-Pro team in 2009. He was also selected to the AFC Pro Bowl teams in 2007 and 2009.

"They took me for granted until I had to pull the trigger."
—Former Browns owner Art Modell, on moving the team to Baltimore

"They took me for granted until I had to pull the trigger," he said.

Cleveland was without professional football for three years. The NFL granted the city an expansion team in 1999, and a new stadium was built. In addition, the league allowed the team to keep its nickname, colors, and official history.

The Browns returned in 1999. But those who expected the glory days to return were in for disappointment.

CLEVELAND'S JOSH CRIBBS RUNS AGAINST PITTSBURGH ON DECEMBER 10, 2009. AS OF 2010, CRIBBS WAS THE NFL'S ALL-TIME LEADER IN KICKOFF RETURNS FOR TOUCHDOWNS.

A series of poor decisions, including a number of bad draft selections, kept Cleveland near the bottom of the standings almost every season through 2009. The Browns failed to achieve consistency during that time, bringing in new coaches and overhauling their team every few years.

From 1999 through 2009, the Browns compiled a lowly record of 59–117. They reached the playoffs only in 2002, losing in the first round. During that stretch, they managed just two winning records in 11 seasons.

The Browns did show some signs of life in 2009, winning their last four games. Owner Randy Lerner added to the optimism by luring Mike Holmgren to become team president.

Holmgren had been to the Super Bowl three times as a head coach of the Green Bay Packers and the Seattle Seahawks. He took over the hiring of coaches and signing of new players.

MORE FRUSTRATION

It appeared that the Browns were going to win in their first playoff game since their return to town. On January 5, 2003, they led the host Pittsburgh Steelers 33–21 in the fourth quarter. Two touchdown passes from Kelly Holcomb to Dennis Northcutt helped Cleveland take that lead. Holcomb would finish with a big game, going 26-for-43 for 429 yards and three touchdowns. But Browns fans had grown accustomed to disappointment, and they were to be disappointed again. The Steelers scored two late touchdowns and defeated the Browns 36–33. Pittsburgh, Cleveland's biggest rival, enjoyed a particularly dominant stretch in the series, winning 18 of 19 meetings between the two teams until falling to the Browns late in the 2009 season.

CLEVELAND BROWNS STADIUM OPENED ON SEPTEMBER 12, 1999. THE NFL GRANTED CLEVELAND AN EXPANSION TEAM THAT BEGAN PLAY IN 1999 WITH THE OLD BROWNS NICKNAME.

"[I am] looking forward to the challenge of not necessarily rebuilding the Browns, because the Browns have a wonderful, wonderful history, but being a part of getting the team back to where they should be. And I'm talking about the playoffs and potentially the Super Bowl."
—Mike Holmgren, after he was named the Browns' president in December 2009

In his first news conference with the Cleveland media, Holmgren spoke about not only returning the Browns to their glory days, but taking it one step further.

"[I am] looking forward to the challenge of not necessarily rebuilding the Browns, because the Browns have a wonderful, wonderful history, but being a part of getting the team back to where they should be," he said. "And I'm talking about the playoffs and potentially the Super Bowl."

MIKE HOLMGREN, HIRED AS THE BROWNS' PRESIDENT IN LATE 2009, WAS INTENT ON IMPROVING THE TEAM.

TIMELINE

1944	The Browns are founded as an AAFC franchise by owner Arthur McBride. Paul Brown is the first coach and runs the organization.
1946	The host Browns win the first AAFC title on December 22 by defeating the New York Yankees 14–9.
1949	The Browns earn a clean sweep of AAFC championships by winning their fourth straight before the league folds. Cleveland defeats the visiting San Francisco 49ers 21–7 on December 11.
1950	The Browns crush the defending champion Philadelphia Eagles 35–10 in their first NFL game. The Browns win the NFL crown with a 30–28 home victory over the Los Angeles Rams on December 24.
1954	After losing two straight years to Detroit in the NFL title game, the host Browns rout the Lions 56–10 for the championship on December 26. Otto Graham throws for three touchdowns and runs for three more.
1955	The Browns capture their second NFL title in a row with a 38–14 road victory over the Rams on December 26. It was Graham's last game, as he retired after the season.
1957	The Browns draft running back Jim Brown, who blossoms into perhaps the greatest player in NFL history.
1964	The Browns win their last title on December 27, defeating the heavily favored Baltimore Colts 27–0 in Cleveland.
1968	The Browns defeat the Dallas Cowboys to reach the NFL Championship Game. But they fall 34–0 to the visiting Colts on December 29 with a Super Bowl berth on the line.

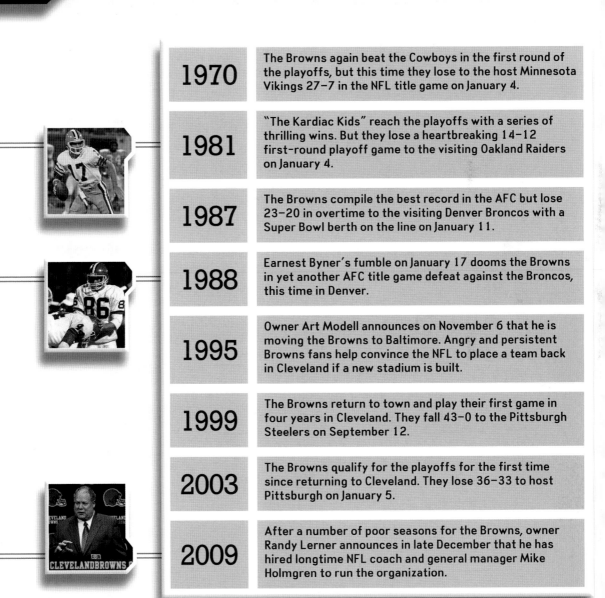

1970	The Browns again beat the Cowboys in the first round of the playoffs, but this time they lose to the host Minnesota Vikings 27–7 in the NFL title game on January 4.
1981	"The Kardiac Kids" reach the playoffs with a series of thrilling wins. But they lose a heartbreaking 14–12 first-round playoff game to the visiting Oakland Raiders on January 4.
1987	The Browns compile the best record in the AFC but lose 23–20 in overtime to the visiting Denver Broncos with a Super Bowl berth on the line on January 11.
1988	Earnest Byner's fumble on January 17 dooms the Browns in yet another AFC title game defeat against the Broncos, this time in Denver.
1995	Owner Art Modell announces on November 6 that he is moving the Browns to Baltimore. Angry and persistent Browns fans help convince the NFL to place a team back in Cleveland if a new stadium is built.
1999	The Browns return to town and play their first game in four years in Cleveland. They fall 43–0 to the Pittsburgh Steelers on September 12.
2003	The Browns qualify for the playoffs for the first time since returning to Cleveland. They lose 36–33 to host Pittsburgh on January 5.
2009	After a number of poor seasons for the Browns, owner Randy Lerner announces in late December that he has hired longtime NFL coach and general manager Mike Holmgren to run the organization.

QUICK STATS

FRANCHISE HISTORY
1946–95; 1999–

SUPER BOWLS
None

NFL CHAMPIONSHIP GAMES
(1950–69; wins in bold)
1950, 1951, 1952, 1953, **1954**, **1955**, 1957, **1964**, 1965, 1968, 1969

AAFC CHAMPIONSHIP GAMES
(1946–49; wins in bold)
1946, **1947**, **1948**, **1949**

AFC CHAMPIONSHIP GAMES
(since 1970 AFL-NFL merger)
1986, 1987, 1989

DIVISION CHAMPIONSHIPS
(since 1970 AFL-NFL merger)
1971, 1980, 1985, 1986, 1987, 1989

KEY PLAYERS
(position, seasons with team)
Jim Brown (RB, 1957–65)
Len Ford (DE, 1950–57)
Frank Gatski (C, 1946–56)
Otto Graham (QB, 1946–55)
Lou Groza (OT/K, 1946–59, 1961–67)
Leroy Kelly (RB, 1964–73)
Bernie Kosar (QB, 1985–93)
Dante Lavelli (WR, 1946–56)
Clay Matthews (LB, 1978–93)
Marion Motley (RB, 1946–53)
Ozzie Newsome (TE, 1978–90)
Brian Sipe (QB, 1974–83)
Paul Warfield (WR, 1964–69,
    1976–77)

KEY COACHES
Paul Brown (1946–62):
    158–48–8; 9–5 (playoffs)
Blanton Collier (1963–70):
    76–34–2; 3–4 (playoffs)

HOME FIELDS
Cleveland Browns Stadium (1999–)
Municipal Stadium (1946–95)

* All statistics through 2009 season

QUOTES AND ANECDOTES

Browns veterans played a practical joke on rookies for many years. Before every Thanksgiving, they told all the rookies that they could get a free turkey. They claimed that there was one for each of them, but they had to drive well out into the country to get it. The rookies were even given driving directions. But when they arrived at that site, they discovered that there were no turkeys anywhere!

Who was the last Browns player to win the NFL Most Valuable Player award? It was quarterback Brian Sipe, who captured it for leading the team to the playoffs in 1980.

Coincidentally, the Browns once had a defensive lineman named Cleveland Crosby. One day he showed up to a meeting wearing a T-shirt bearing the name of the Browns' hated rivals, the Pittsburgh Steelers. Coach Sam Rutigliano forced Crosby to remove the shirt and sit in the meeting bare-chested.

One of the smallest players in Browns history was kick returner Gerald (Ice Cube) McNeil. When McNeil arrived for his first day of practice in 1986, he asked team publicist Dino Lucarelli for tickets for his family and friends. "I'm sorry," Lucarelli replied. "I can only get tickets for players." "I am a player," McNeil said. "I'm Gerald McNeil." Lucarelli later confessed that he thought McNeil was a ball boy. After all, McNeil was just 5-foot-7 and weighed 140 pounds.

GLOSSARY

American Football League

A professional football league that operated from 1960 to 1969 before merging with the National Football League.

blossom

To quickly or gradually become a much better player.

comeback

Coming from behind to take a lead in a particular game.

dominant

The player or team that proves to be consistently better than an opponent.

franchise

An entire sports organization, including the players, coaches, and staff.

legendary

Well known and admired over a long period.

mediocre

Neither good nor bad.

momentum

A continued strong performance based on recent success.

negotiate

To work out a business arrangement.

retire

To officially end one's career.

rookie

A first-year professional athlete.

secondary

The defensive players who line up behind the linebackers to defend the pass and assist with run coverage.

showdown

A long-anticipated battle between two good or great players or teams.

sidearm

The release of a ball from the side of the body.

sure-handed

Referring to a receiver who rarely drops passes.

FOR MORE INFORMATION

Further Reading

Grossi, Tony. *Tales From the Browns Sideline*. Champaign, IL: Sports Publishing LLC, 2004.

Keim, John. *Legends by the Lake (Ohio History and Culture)*. Akron, OH: University of Akron Press, 1999.

Sports Illustrated. *The Football Book Expanded Edition*. New York: Sports Illustrated Books, 2009.

Web Links

To learn more about the Cleveland Browns, visit ABDO Publishing Company online at **www.abdopublishing.com**. Web sites about the Browns are featured on our Book Links page. These links are routinely monitored and updated to provide the most current information available.

Places to Visit

Cleveland Browns Stadium
1085 West 3rd Street
Cleveland, OH 44114
440-891-5001
www.clevelandbrowns.com/tickets/stadium
The Browns play their home exhibition, regular-season, and playoff games here.

Cleveland Browns Training and Administrative Complex
76 Lou Groza Boulevard
Berea, OH 44017
440-891-5000
www.clevelandbrowns.com/team/facility.php
Practices are open to the public during training camp in August. The Browns also practice here during the season.

Pro Football Hall of Fame
2121 George Halas Drive Northwest
Canton, OH 44708
330-456-8207
www.profootballhof.com
This hall of fame and museum highlights the greatest players and moments in the history of the National Football League. As of 2010, 21 people affiliated with the Browns had been enshrined, including Jim Brown, Paul Brown, Otto Graham, and Ozzie Newsome.

INDEX

About the Author

Marty Gitlin is a freelance writer based in Cleveland, Ohio. He has written more than 25 educational books. Gitlin has won more than 45 awards during his 25 years as a writer, including first place for general excellence from the Associated Press. He lives with his wife and three children.